~10th August 1859

I have often thought how
much I would like to keep
a journal of my every day
life in England.

Published by
REARDON PUBLISHING
56 Upper Norwood Street, Leckhampton,
Cheltenham, Glos, GL53 0DU
England, UK, EU
website: www.reardon.co.uk

Published for
Sudeley Castle Estates
in association with Douglas Barrett
Copyright 1998

Fully Revised Second
Edition 1999

Line upon Line Gibraltar

ISBN 1 873877 28 5

Layout and Design
Nicholas Reardon

Printed by
Stoate and Bishop Printers
Cheltenham Glos

An Introduction
by
LADY ASHCOMBE

Emma Dent's presence began to assert itself almost as soon as I took over responsibility for Sudeley Castle in the early 1970's . Everywhere I looked there was nothing this extraordinary woman had not had a hand in. Her achievements at Sudeley and in Winchcombe and its environs left a daunting and salutary example of Victorian philanthropy. My image of her was a stern and intimidating matriarch. It was not until years later, when I discovered her diaries that a softer, more intriguing truth was revealed. Here was a woman with a wry sense of humour, a deep enduring love for her husband and a fiercely unconvential streak. Often alone and suffering from an oppressive sense of duty, she seemed happiest when travelling.

Besides her diaries a wealth of personal items, scrapbooks and trunks full of lace and needlework remained tucked away in the old 'Long Room', (where the exhibition is now housed) unexplored for three-quarters of a century. I felt an interesting tribute to Emma's life at Sudeley could be created from this odd assortment of memorabilia.

I'm grateful to Douglas Barrett for his interest and for his help in putting together this project which resulted in "The Lace and Times of Emma Dent". The surfeit of material forced us to be very selective in choosing the quotes. I hope you enjoy reading them as much as we enjoyed finding them.

Selected Writings
from the
Journals of Emma Dent
1851 - 1896

FROM AN EXHIBITION AT SUDELEY CASTLE

~May 1851

On the 26th to Long's Hotel, Bond Street, for a few weeks in London for the first Great Exhibition! My journal full of notes and admiration - a sight it certainly was which we have never seen surpassed in any of our foreign wanderings.

~8th May 1851

Philip spent the day with us - we went to the Chinese exhibition - and to see Tom Thumb - that miserable dwarf.

~June 4th 1851

I suffered very much indeed from my heart - frightful spasms which held me down - sometimes for twenty minutes - so that I could not move. The first I had was in my sleep and I dreamt that Death came with his dart and touched my heart - I woke in the acutest pain.

~July 2nd 1851

Martin Dent, John's brother, arrived in England from Australia.

~August 8th 1851

I performed "The Dwarf" for a party of children at the Philpotts, younger in those days! I was never tired of playing with and amusing children - what scenes of gypsies and robbers - we used to get up to in the Severn Bank Woods - a great trick was to dress up a figure to represent myself and pretend to be sitting on the battlements on the top of the house, then disappear at the same moment the figure fell over into the garden.

~November 17th 1852

A fine day decided us to go to London for the Duke's Funeral! On the 18th by six o'clock we were at the Conservative Club. Nothing could have been more interesting, solemn and impressive than the procession and the respect paid to the remains of Arthur Duke of Wellington as they were borne along the street to his resting place in Westminster Abbey!

It was very cold sitting and waiting at the open window for so many hours on that November morning, but the sun shone - bright and warm rays fell on the procession as it slowly and mournfully passed down St. James's Street - it was a day of real hero worship - such as we shall never see again!

~1855

Martin was buried at Sudeley - it seems but yesterday I was watching him standing over the grave of his Uncle William and now, like a shadow, he has himself followed - so, like a dream or a tale that is told we follow the generations of our fathers!

Now that he is gone how little we seem to have left to remind us of his very eventful life - the portrait of Gen. Wolf in the Library by Sir Joshua Reynolds was purchased because of its extraordinary likeness to him - and in my museum I presume some of the first daguerreotypes of the natives ever bought to England. A few nuggets of gold of his own finding - his permit to dig - and the skull of a native woman who was killed in a foray with an English party!

~1856

The first wild bursting of the heart to Heaven, and its cramping, crushing, afterwards.

~February 15th 1856

Gilbert Scott, John and headman consulting all morning about stables.

~April 13th 1856
My last Sunday in Severnstoke Church. Mr. Burrows preached. I was quite sad to see so many familiar faces for the last time. The faces of my dear poor people - God help them all!! Tho' I have worked hard among them, how, little I have accomplished!

~April 15th 1856
John and I have had long and very serious talks over the past - ending in many good and noble resolutions for the future - entering on our new and enlarged sphere of usefulness we go with a most sincere trust of God giving us strength to do our duty!

~April 21st 1856
I took my final departure such a lovely, bright, clear fresh morning.

~June 7th 1856
Mr. Gilbert Scott, the architect came to arrange for the restoration of the Chapel. It was an anxious morning for I somehow still clung to the hope that even at the eleventh hour it might be averted - I was sorry for Mr Scott for I could see he was puzzled to know what to do for the best - and grieved to give the order to scrape the walls and denude them of their exquisite greys, and moss and roses, and wallflowers and elder trees!

~June 17th 1856
I am very anxious Sudeley Chapel should not be restored! Contrary to the opinions I know, of all good people. In my anxiety I was so bold as to write to Ruskin for his opinion - which came today in a very interesting letter - he recommends NO restoration! "A pile of mossy stones, a fitter monument for Queen Katherine Parr, than the most gorgeous church that wealth could erect!"

~July 3rd 1856
MB. and I have finished the Chinese Room! After two or three hard days work papering and patching - for the paper was too short - and we had to cut pieces out and paste them on at the bottom to make it sufficiently long - we took it in turns to ascend the ladder and it was charming work arranging colours for the the doors.

When the great bedstead was put in its place it seemed quite to crowd and spoil the room.

~September 1st 1856
A long letter waiting for me from our friend Holme Cardwell, the sculptor, to say he has just sent off from Rome our statue of Sabrina!

~10th August 1859
I have often thought how much I would like to keep a journal of my every day life in England.

~30th September 1859
I was very busy arranging patchwork for the curtains of the old oak bedstead with the Royal Arms, which we have just had restored and put up in our own room - the needlework in the room will be all my own doing.

~16th November 1859
Mr. Henry Coventry also stayed with us during their visit. We gave two little dinner parties in the same week - and had the Folls who have lately purchased that interesting old place, Beckford Hall. We have come to the conclusion that the Hall is more interesting than the occupants.

~December 1859
Lord S. took me into dinner, and very much he puzzled me in his style of conversation - pretending to know nothing, referring to Mr. Holland constantly for confirmation of all he said, and if he is what he pretends to be, he is one of the most empty headed, bloated aristocrats I have the pleasure of knowing! Lady Sudeley is a very gentle, kind, good little woman and their eldest daughter Julia very amiable and nice.

~December 1859
Our cousin Julius Brenchley has been staying with us - after all these years it was very pleasant to meet again and talk over old merry times. He has been a great traveller - indeed I hardly know where he has not been - and strange habits too and tastes he has acquired.

He says he really prefers raw fish to cooked, and has constantly eaten game uncooked - once amongst the savages he was forced to eat a piece of human flesh!

~26th December 1859
The servants had a party consisting of husbands, wives, and children. Marianne and I for their amusement dressed up; she in the Bears Dress and I as old Christmas - we made an appearance on the balcony of the Servant's Hall and were greeted with thundering applause. We lowered Christmas presents amongst them and disappeared as we had appeared.

~23rd January 1860
Staying in the house we had Sir Maxwell and Lady Steele, Mr. & Miss Marriott, Mary Thompson, Hon. Tom Coventry and his nephew Mr. Henry Coventry. This last has paid marked attention to my sister all winter, so much so that everyone is remarking and commenting upon his devotion and how it will end!

~3rd February 1860
Poor Marianne and I find the hours going very anxiously - for a great, the greatest event, in her life has happened:-
Henry Coventry came on Monday to take leave of her - he stayed here the night - next day she and Bessie Calrow went to the Alderton Quarries; when they were gone he told me how long, how many years he had loved my sister ! and implored me to tell him had he any hope of having his love returned?

~11th February 1860
More than six weeks have passed and nothing has been settled in favour of Henry Coventry and Marianne's engagement. My father won't hear of it! Nothing that we can say has any effect. Marianne I cannot understand, all I feel is that a beautiful future is clouded, a mirror broken never to be joined. I saw H.C. a few days ago, and I was obliged to tell him my father's objections were not only on the score of want of property but that the Coventry family generally were not such as he would have his daughter marry into - even the present young Earl is already so much on the Turf!! It was a very hard interview. I believe that there is still the bitterest disappointment in store for him!

from Grenada to Manzanares

140 miles – same boy all the way –

From Grenada to Manzanares
140 miles - same boy all the way -

~6th April 1860

I have been much interested in trying experiments on a gyroscope a new invention by a Frenchman - it goes to prove that inertia is a property of matter in motion as well as of matter in rest, that orbital and axial motions are connected and may regulate each other. It is a beautiful scientific plaything.

~14th April 1860

I heard of Cousin Pattie's engagement to Dr. Phillips of Manchester, it seems it has been a long engagement, or rather attachment, that Uncle Tom would not hear of it for a long time on account of his profession, and no means of settlements - but finally he has given his consent, and with it £15,000 as Pattie's dowry - and so I wish them every happiness and can only hope that "our stern Parent" may relent in the same manner!

The last two days there has been a great excitement in the garden, planting the yew alleys - it is like magic to see these beautiful trees in already - 10 or 12ft high, furnishing the grounds more than we could possibly have imagined. We must hope they will live, and do the garden credit:- I quite long to see them cut into form.

~10th May 1860

I HAVE SEEN THE EMPEROR ! ! ! The greatest man of his age, he was in an open carriage with the Empress - driving in the Bois de Boulogne. His eagle like eyes were directed towards us, and he smiled and raised his hat. He is much better looking than I expected to see him, he is not like his portraits - no portrait could be truthful, for his expression seemed to change several times during the few seconds that we saw him.

~14th May 1860

Mon. Traitt gave me notice that the Emperor was going to call on a friend of his, Compte d'Agrarde in the Place Vendome. The Compte is an amateur photographer and they were all going to be photographed. The Compte is going to be married to one of the ladies of the court, and there is great difficulty how to break the news to his chere amie, Mrs. Hope, living only a few doors off, but the Confesseur is to do it! Mrs. Hope being of so violent a temperament they dread what may be the consequences.

~26th May 1860
A letter from Papa and telegraphic message that Philip had been dangerously ill - but was better - and then we took another carriage - and away to Pau - nearly 70 miles in 7 hours - good posting - beautiful roads - no view owing to the mist - so gave my mind to Dicken's new and wonderful book "Tale of Two Cities".

~30th May 1860
I had intended to have written down so many thoughts, so many feelings tonight, but I am so sad I can only record my sorrow!

~31st May 1860
From Eaux Chaudes to Lourdes. On approaching Lourdes our coachman pointed out where the Virgin appeared to some children in a grotto.

~26th August 1860
It is nearly two months since I recorded anything in my journal. Marianne has quite broken off her engagement with Henry Coventry - when I last saw him he was broken hearted.

This evening John was coming to me to read to me Ruskin's last volume, when I very unnecessarily found fault with him for playing with and spoiling a paper cutter I intended for a prize - he became impatient - words followed he left the room - but returned in a few minutes. The chapter he was going to read in Ruskin's book was on "PEACE".

~9th September 1860
John laid up with rheumatic gout - I have a little iron bedstead in the dressing room, and last night with the blind up, as I could not sleep I watched the stars - and I know not why or how, but the little bedstead took me back a long time ago, when I was a child living with the Brunos at 27 Euston Place, and then I had just such another little bedstead.

~16th September 1860

Our wedding day thirteen years ago! It rained then - it rains now - a dreary day truly as far as exteriors are concerned - John still laid up with rheumatism - I am much interested in a new book called "Recreations of a Country Parson" by Boyd, a Scotsman, it commends the keeping of a Diary, recording work and how our hours are spent - what a splendid diary mine would be! For example on Friday, waiting on the invalid, and studying Spanish, Chapter of Orlandorff till 11.30, stitch, stitch, at the 6th angel for the Altar Cloth till 2 o'clock dinner time - more Spanish - inclination to headache - went out - called at the red brick cottage - talked to the eldest girl, got her to promise to be industrious, to clear up before her mother came home from reaping; and then walked to Humblebee Cottage - paid Alice Bolton a long visit, promised her 6 yards of flannel and odds and ends for filling pillows - called also next door, admired the baby, increased cleanliness etc., then on to the tenants at Wadfield Farm - looked at their alterations in kitchen and passages, chatted a few minutes with the stone masons, and so home. Had tea at six - read for an hour - prepared patchwork for school children - headache so much worse went to bed early.

~Saturday - September 1860

Spent in waiting on John - working at Altar Cloth - Spanish - a visit from Mr. Traill and Fred Holland - writing to inquire about Nurse's Institution at Liverpool - reading Italian Testament and Gerusalemme Liberata - Recreations of a Country Parson - preparing patchwork, and so, very tired to bed. Call that work! How much is said and written about work nowadays - I wish someone would write a book and define work! And give women in such circumstances as I am more difficult work to do!

~Tuesday - January 1861

Miss Francis and I all morning arranging books for the prizes in Girls Sunday School. At night poor Mary Summers called - she was in a very excited state - more mad than anyone I ever saw - to tell me her sister was dead at the Gloucester Asylum - and might she be buried at the Castle - anywhere - in or outside - anywhere handy! It was her sister's request before she went to the Asylum.

In spite of the frost, and drifted snow, and East wind, I took Mr. & Mrs. Osborne to Monks Hole, Hayle's Abbey, and home by the road - a tremendous walk, and we thought ourselves great heroes. We started at 2.30 and did not get back till 10 minutes after 6.00.

~2nd April 1861

I began wood sawing, and to my great surprise accomplished a little book stand with only breaking two saws, but they are very fine - 6d a dozen - and the frame cost 7/6d.

~9th April 1861

We dined at Dumbleton - the sailor boy is now at home - Henry Coventry was there - looking worn and older, they say he is ill, and much changed, and indeed he looks so!

~9th April 1861

They are making the walk before the Chapel door and planting the hedge of yews. In the Chapel they are busy putting down the flooring, and yesterday K. Parr's leaden coffin was moved for the last time - and her remains - (A Little Brown Dust) - put into the new tomb!

~11th April 1861

I think it is one of my greatest blessings to be able to say I never know what it is to feel dull or lonely ! but in society have often thought "oh when will this be over"!

~25th May 1861

In the sunshine, as the clock struck mid-day, John and I, and Bayliss the maid, started on our travels - it seemed a few days ago as if it would be impossible to bring ones little worldly affairs to a close, and make arrangements for leaving home - but by dint of hard work and late hours the last arrangement was at last made, the final order given, and as we rolled away I thought how soon, in five minutes perhaps the domestic world would cease to regret us - and I could not help thinking how like it all is to life and death - we fancy the world will stand still without us, our little world at least, and all our little plans will come to nought when we are gone - but is it so? The time for our long journey thro' the Dark Valley comes - we hurry our arrangements, we leave injunctions to some - loving remembrances to a few, (How few when there are so many to love) - and at our departure others with fresher spirits take up our work - ere the passing bell has ceased to toll, the keen regret is over and we are hardly remembered - Oh! how with such thoughts as these can any of us be proud!

~5th June 1861
Cavour died this morning at 7 o'clock - a sad event for Italy.

~July 1861
Beer - the artist mixes his colours in beer - the dullest become enthusiastic on the subject of beer - Munich has a name for being a very dissolute city - but there is some sort of law which prevents people from marrying unless they have a certain sum to live upon, the consequence is half the population is illegitimate - besides beer drinking a great deal of dancing goes on amongst the lower orders, but in a decorous sort of way, and if a stranger went in and took any kind of liberty he would be kicked out immediately.

It has been a great pleasure to go thro' the old Pinacothek - many of the pictures I remembered, and it seems strange how much my taste has changed - how the Carlo Dolas have gone out and the Hemlings come in.

~July 1861
The earnest, eloquent, soulful woman who wrote Aurora Leigh is dead - Elizabeth Barrett Browning ! The fair climate of Italy could not ward off the Destroyer. Flowers and sunshine, blue skies and purple hills, fruits and purling streams - what are they all against Death?

~August 1861
The comet which is called the Garibaldi Comet, and which we first saw the Eve we were at Olten seems to astonish and surprise the astronomers - Lavernier of the French Academy of Science

acknowledges that they know nothing of it, and it is the first time it has visited us.

~August 1861

The fire near London Bridge is talked of as being the most awful that has occurred since the Great Fire of 1666. The head fireman, Braidwood, was burnt in it, and at his funeral there was a procession that lasted 3 hours, so much was he respected.

~10th August 1861

We have been very much interested in the account by Russell of the Bull's Run fight in America where the Southerners put to ignominious flight the Northerners.

~28th August 1861

Mrs. Holland showed me her sewing machine, and how it worked, a wonderful American invention by which yards of work may be done in a few minutes. Mr. Fred has lately come from Egypt and the Holy Land and is now going to take a curacy and settle down to work.

~15th December 1861

The astounding news of the death of Prince Albert was telegraphed to Macclesfield - that he died last nigh of gastric fever - only 42!

We have postponed our fancy party owing to Prince Albert's death for a month - it is little we can do, to show our feeling for our beloved Queen, and the least is to postpone such like festivities till the first few weeks of mourning are over.

~January 1862

Beautiful carvings, windows, and marble floors - Scott, Phillip & Preedy have done their best - and already their names seem more associated with it than Cromwell and his soldiers. Pleased as I am that the Chapel has been so exquisitely restored, and that it was perhaps our duty not to leave the House of God in ruins. Still I cannot help regretting deeply & sincerely that the historical record must of necessity, now be quickly obliterated. I am reading now to the servants on Sunday nights.

Lord Hamilton sale going on - K. Parr by Holbein sold for £800 gs. John bid to 790 gs. Colnaghi and he contested neck and neck from 600 - it was said Colnaghi got it on commission for Lord Leconfield - but I am heartily glad we did not get it, as I think we have done our duty to that lamented Queen!

Seville, Summer 1862

The Plaza del Toros - lately built and considered the finest in Spain. The first matador in Spain was killed last Sunday in Madrid! The Valencians are the most blood thirsty of the Spanish and they delight in these exhibitions. Last year he saw a Matador stuck in the back by the bull and tossed into the midst of the spectators. He said they will sell their beds to go to the bullfights! It is the great National amusement.

The doors of the bulls' stalls out of which they come tearing and snorting like wild beasts - when killed he becomes the property of the Matador - it is truly a barbarous sport!

It begins to be very hot in the middle of the day and we found it boiling on our way to the manufacturing of tobacco - the men were just leaving for dinner - they were all searched as they went out - shoes taken off, scarves unwound, hats raised. The first process was grinding the plant into powder for tobacco, then we went into a room where women and children were making up the little paper boxes to contain tobacco - then they weighed and filled them. In an enormous room where they were making cigars, the women cut open the bundles of tobacco, rolled it into shape, took a good leaf, rolled the cigar in it, put a touch of gum at one end to keep the point from opening, measured it according to a mark on the table, cut it the right length and the cigar was finished! This establishment employs 8,000 women, 1,000 men some of the women were perfectly beautiful. All had roses in their hair and they work from 6.00 am to 8.00 pm and receive from 4 to 10 reals a day.

~London 1862

The last morning we were in town we went to Silvy (the best photographer, they say, in London). Silvy would not allow us to have a voice of our own in arranging positions and as he persisted in taking the crooked side of my face I expect to come out as bad as ever.

~Sunday 14th 1862

There is a curious story told of the American War. The Confederate General Morgan was making a kind of foray and was at a point on the Louisville and Nashville railroad when the brilliant idea occurred to him to cut the telegraph wires, and by means of a pocket apparatus, belonging to someone with him, they contrived to stop the enemy's messages and return to them incorrect answers!

~26th September 1862

Our annual tea party - 360 children including National Sunday Union & cottagers' children - 15 male and 17 female teachers - all the farmers wives and daughters- and a great number of visitors - a most beautiful day - though raining in the morning.

~October 30th 1862

We have been again to the Great International Exhibition - it appears to me more wonderful and interesting each time I see it. A collection of all that is most interesting from all corners of the Globe, united and classified under one roof.

~November 2nd 1862

We went to Westminster Abbey for afternoon service - most beautifully conducted - the chanting and organ magnificent.

I had not been in Westminster Abbey since as a girl at the Queen's Coronation. (1837)

I remember my father and mother were staying in Maddox Street, I was there for a holiday from lessons at the Brunos (27 Euston Place, New Road!) and my father came in about 11.00 at night and brought the joyful intelligence that he had got tickets for me and Jane Gaskell for the East Gallery over the Nave. Long before it was light we were at the gates waiting to go in with the first rush at 8 o'clock, and good places we had! Looking down the nave the side aisles where sat the Peers and Peeresses! and our then young and lovely Queen before the altar - oh what an effecting and glorious sight it was!! I remember the crown catching in her hair at one part of the ceremony, when she had to take it off and place it on the altar, and how Lord Roll, I think was his name, tripped up the steps as he went up to the throne to pay obeisance (he was very old and feeble) and how he fell a second time, and then the Queen with a natural impulse rushed forward to assist him and then the thunder of applause that followed - it was deafening and brought tears to many eyes. Then I shall never forget the God Save the Queen!

~6th November 1862
I got from Speilmann, the money changer in the City some foreign coins, with an intention of making a collection of current coins. Also Heaton of the Birmingham mint send me some paper impressions of coins of out of the way places, such as Venezuela, Siam, and Persia. It seems curious that we should make coins for foreign countries.

My father talked a great deal this evening about death and how easily his own father died at the age of 82. I think he was as well as usual, had dined and asked his wife or daughter to read a Psalm, while they were reading he fell asleep and never woke again.

~4th May 1863
I was delighted with Mr. Young an enthusiastic and good talker on all subjects. The conversation turned principally on the marvellous, and he told us some marvellous stories. One was that many years ago on a Tuesday night he woke up, felt wide awake and heard in a sepulchral voice repeated so often that it quite haunted him, "Dowdeswell Pull Court", names he declares he had never heard in his life. On Wednesday he called on the Miss Smiths and the excellent Mr Robinson of Brighton was also there (it was at Brighton this occurred). Their conversation turned on dreams, when Mr. Young related his previous night's dream. They laughed and said there was nothing marvellous in it and the names were unknown to them all, but on Thursday the first thing they saw in the paper was "died on Tuesday Mr. Dowdeswell of Pull Court"

The wonderful part of the story was that the spirit of Dowdeswell should have spoken to a man who had never even heard of him, but many months after Mr. Young accidentally heard that Dowdeswell had been in the habit of frequenting that very house, and that there might have been reasons for a departing spirit to mourn there.

~Sunday 10th May 1863
The week has flown - working on my knees in the morning at the restoration of the Roman pavement in the greenhouse.

~October 6th 1863
In the night between 3 and 4 o'clock an earthquake was felt, nearly all over England - no one here felt it but in Winchcombe and the neighbourhood all who felt it compared it to "like someone under the bed". In Cheltenham the policeman noticed the houses rock and the trees of the Promenade shake as if from the roots.

~Sunday Evening December 1863
I am beginning my autograph book and it promises well with the Duke of Wellington, Garibaldi, and Paganini - by way of a beginning.

Bishop of Columbia - at 3'oclock we went up to the National School - and I was much gratified in seeing so large an audience- the Bishop gave a most interesting address and spoke for 2 hours and a quarter. The collection was £22.10.0 which we all thought excellent and I trust with the blessing of God Almighty the interest which he excited in us for the Columbia Mission may be long kept alive in our hearts!

After the meeting we had tea handed round and a few remained to be introduced to the Bishop. At dinner he talked to us about his work at Yarmouth and how he had been to see them since his return to England. How there were 3,000 persons present at his preaching and how they all waited to shake hands with him!

~11th January 1864
We dined with the Traitts at la Bonnefoy restaurant in Montmartre

and then spent the remainder of the evening with them at their home and with their amusing children. They showed me their stamp books and begged me to remember them in that line at Constantinople! There is a complete rage as in England for collecting stamps. To my fancy a most uninteresting one as to the collector, they neither give the pleasure of association nor beauty. In Paris the exchange was carried to such a pitch amongst the children that the gardens of the Tuileries were called "La Petite Bourse" and the police at last forbade them buying and selling the stamps.

~Rome, Spring 1864

I took a lesson in mosaic working from a friend of Mr. Cardwell's, Rubicondi, via Felice, and he is to send me prepared and ready for me to continue a copy of a cross in St. Peters which I hope to put up in the Sudeley Chapel. John has written to Mr. Scott the architect to suggest having him in England to work on Prince Albert's tomb.

~Italy, Spring 1864

Pompei - there we had to pay 2frs. each to go in and clicked thro' a round turnstile as in the Great Exhibition.

The frescoes recently discovered were very bright, brilliant yellow and red, all treasures are taken to the museum. The beautiful gold lamp was found in the new part but the most sad, the most interesting story is suggested by the skeletons. One is in the room where money and treasures were found!
Two women, one lying with her head on her hand and with the impression of a handkerchief on the lava, as if she had tried to save herself from suffocation, the legs contorted as if in agony. The other women appeared in attitudes of despair - there were also skeletons of poor dogs. Pompei looked more than ever the city of the dead - the streets so quiet and deserted! and the world we saw thro the ruined arches and beyond, so full of life, so bright and grand and beautiful! and there was the great destroying mountain looking so innocent, without a vestige of smoke or fire, looking down, as if it were placidly on its work of horror, and when we left we stopped at the little Albergo outside (consisting only of a

kitchen and a ladder that led to an upper room) and had biscuits and wine before the door waited upon by a little hunchbacked man and two bright eyed fine looking women who all looked so pleasantly at us because I said " Viva il vostro bel paese".
And as we sat at the door we could see Vesuvius thro' the kitchen - oh what a picture it was!

~Constantinople Spring 1864
We crossed in a caique to Scutari! It was very rough and we were very thankful to land.

Landing in Asia was a great event in our travels! Wild looking men and horses were waiting to be hired, but we walked, under Mr. Marshall's guidance, thro' the town, miserable and curious looking enough.A long walk to the Howling Dervishes! at their convent-their place of worship is a square room with curious looking things hung around. The most curious part of their performance is when they all stand close together exclaiming sacred sentences-bending to the right, forward, backward, to the left, again and again, and as quickly as possible-they looked mad.

~April 25th 1864
Two days and nearly two nights travelling by Diligence from Boulogne to Paris. I thought it wonderfully delightful then and am not sure if it were not for the nightwork if I should not greatly prefer the "old way" to the uninteresting new, even now. In this railway travelling, there is positively nothing to be seen from the time we get in to the time we get out.

John in Paris called on Mr. Evans (the Emperor's dentist) whose acquaintance we made on the Danube.

He took John a drive in the Bois de Boulogne. The Emperor bowed to him, the Empress waved her hand, the Little Prince shouted out to him, beautiful ladies smiled, and he pointed out to John all the most distinguished personages. They were finally run into by a runaway horse and had a narrow escape with only a broken shaft - he told John he had looked down the throats of nearly all the crowned heads in Europe! and gave us seals and monograms that he had received on letters from Royalty.

~11th August 1864 - Scotland
I left the gentlemen to continue their route to the Moors, Cotterstone. I and Bayliss came on to Kelso to join Marianne and Miss Booth. I found them in very humble lodgings, with a very strong mixture of bad smells arising from their photographic chemicals.

~16th August 1864 - Scotland
We came to Melrose - got comfortable lodgings at one Yules a Tailor - the M.B.'s pitched their photographic tent in the Abbey and worked all afternoon. What a funny couple they looked as they walked on in front, both dressed alike, very small hats without veils, very thick sailor coats, showing no white collars, old black silk dresses well looped up - Miss Booth's looped up with leather straps - thick boots, nothing in their hands, many turned to look after them and smiled!

~27th August 1864
Marianne and Miss Booth seemed to be all in all to one another. I felt quite jealous and it required great determination to "smother" the nasty little mean green eyed monster - I wonder if it is only natural, or whether it is very bad in me to have such feelings - we used to be so all in all to one another & now I am quite the third!

~31st August 1864
Part of the journey I was quite alone, then a gentleman got in, and owing to the horrible things now of so frequent an occurrence in railway carriages we were absurdly shy of one another - till others got in and pleasant conversation became general.

~29th December 1864
I received a most beautiful letter from Miss Florence Nightingale thanking me so much for my remembrance from Scutari - the little dried flowers she tells me are placed at the foot of the bed where she is now a constant prisoner and the sight of them filled her eyes with tears of joy, and would make her Xmas a day of thanksgiving - she says she is overwhelmed with army business and the trying

part of which is that she may never see the bodies or souls which the work is for but my Scutari flowers are as it were a pledge to the eye of the spirit of the work of our heroes lying at Scutari whose uncomplaining endurance she always strives to be worthy of.

~ January 1865
A dreadful thing has occurred in Winchcombe, Richard Smith, brother to the lawyer, killed his wife on Tuesday night - it seems he shot her about 9 o'clock. Next morning he went up to his sisters at Gloster House & Preston one of the sons came out to him - he said

"Your Mother is Dead"
How?
"The gun went off & killed her"
Did it go off accidentally?

To this he made no reply! She was shot thro' the back of the neck and must have died in a moment - it's a dreadful business for the family.

~October 1865
The strangest thing I ever knew in all my travels and experiences - a young woman preach!!! and it came to pass thro' our seeing an advertisement that Miss Bemrose would preach at 7 o'clock in Jubilee Chapel.

Then our Dinah began her sermon with the text "He that cometh unto me I will in no way cast out" - her voice was most exquisitely touching and soft when she not overstrain it - she preached for nearly an hour - a beautiful sermon - full of tender pleading to bring sinners to Christ - she referred to a custom they, (the primitive Methodists) have of bidding penitents, when they are converted and "wish to have religion" come to the Communion rails- where the Ministers pray for them and there they pray aloud also.

~Wednesday November 8th 1865
All England lamenting the death of Lord Palmerston.

~1866

We have seen the "Lanterne Magique" a long French piece - a review of the past year - not fit for modest women or right minded men to see - they say the French taste is very low just now.

~Ash Wednesday 1866

A quarter of a million sterling given by the American Banker, Mr. Peabody for the creation of lodging houses for the poor in London is one of the most noble gifts of this century - they are to be erected and the poor are to pay for their lodgings a reasonable rent. This rent is again to be spent in erecting more lodgings and so it will go increasing for ever.

~17th June 1866

Mrs. Parker of Little Comberton brought over for the day Mrs. Millais formerly Mr. Ruskin's wife - now the happy wife of Millais & mother of 7 children - a most interesting and delightful person - (Effie Grey) full of conversation and anecdote - had just returned from Italy where she had been travelling with her husband, Mr. Sayard and two other friends

~August 12th 1866

The electric Telegraph is accomplished!

~2nd December 1866

The service all beautifully conducted - sacrament administered - a very good number of communicants - a large congregation in our Sudeley Chapel - a good sermon again from Mr. Jackson.

~18th December 1866

Lord Wemyss told me he once heard two deaf friends of his comparing notes as to the causes of their deafness. The gentleman said he caught his by lying out - she said she got hers from lying in - those precious old dears, the Miss Talbots, especially Miss Jane who said, "Oh those horrid working men I'm quite sick of hearing of the working men!" Alfred Charteris amused us all again very much by doing the tricks of the cut thumb and cracked nose!.

~30th December 1866
John had a shooting party - Mr. Plumbe - Thackwells - Jackson - MB's dined not a pleasant evening.

~7th June 1867
The news is confirmed that the Emperor Maximilian of Mexico has been shot. The grand ceremony in Rome on 29th June of the canonisation and the centenary of St. Peter & Paul passed off very well. The question of the Pope's infallibility is one of the great ones of the day - to be introduced as a dogma!

~24th August 1867
Dined and played at American gambling game of poker!

~January 1st 1868 - Opening of Dent's School
I felt someone ought to say a few words so I said them to the mothers! They were as follows:

"I never made a speech in my life but I feel I must say a few words to you tonight. It gives me very very great pleasure to see you all here and before the amusement begins I should like to say how much I hope you all like the New School prepared for your children - you know that it has been built according to the will and desire of our late good kind uncle Mr. Dent and it has been my husband's great wish to carry out to the letter what he thought would please his uncle - both he and Mr. William Dent have been in my mind all day and over and over again I have wished they could have been amongst us - they were very much interested in Winchcombe and very anxious to do you good - you understand that what was the National School is now divided into two - Miss Malins is coming here with 130 children - the older children. Mr. Smith has kindly consented to let you have his beautiful room for the infants school. On Saturday next a new mistress, Miss Freeman, is coming from the same good college as Miss Malins, to take charge of the infants.

I have thanked Mr. Smith in the name of you all, and do again this evening for his great kindness to you all and liberality in letting you have his School and house for the infants.

I hope you really feel that we are all very anxious to help you in educating your children - I say in helping because the great principle part of education you know must be done in your own homes by your own firesides. In my own heart, I hope you feel that I really love you and your children, and that I feel as if I were your sister placed by God to live near and amongst you to set you a good example and to help you as much as is in my power - I often feel a very great responsibility in living in the big castle and having so many more of the good things of this life than you, and when I hear the voice of God telling me to help my sisters, it always seems as if they are most to be helped by helping their children, and by helping them to become good women, and good wives and mothers when it will be their turn to take your places.

You can help us again to do this by sending them punctually, clean and neat - encouraging them to tell you of what they are learning, taking an interest in their different lessons. Miss Malins desires me to tell you that the bell will ring at five minutes to nine and five to two. Five minutes after nine and two they will not be admitted - also that if a child has been absent for a month it will not be admitted without a good reason given or a fine of a shilling.

Miss Malins has now been working for us for some years and I take this opportunity of saying how pleased and grateful I am to her for the energetic, kind and excellent manner in which she conducts the school. I assure you I never enter it without finding her and all her teachers each in their class hard at work. You can not be grateful enough to her for what she does for your children.
In conclusion let me wish you again to help us by setting them a good example, praying for them, and us and so strengthening the hands of those who teach them, and may God bless you all, fathers and mothers of Winchcombe, and may the children who will be taught in this school grow up to be good Christians, good men and women, to lead good lives in this world, and so prepare for the better life above and thus fulfil the great wish of the founder of this School".

The women were quite tender hearted over it and afterwards I heard quite appreciated my wish to please and encourage them.

France: En Route to Barcelona (with a little too much diligence)

En Route Spain (a little further on)

~17th June 1868

The body of the Emp. Maximilian was brought in by candle and flambeaux.

~18th June 1868

We went to see the coffin lying in State in the Private Chapel.

~21st July 1868

Henry Coventry married Leila Craven - may they be happy!

~24th August 1868

Sudeley's own Baker, John had up before the Magistrates for selling light weighed bread and with alum - fined £8.

~26th August 1868

Donations to Chapel:-
from Uncle Will's Legacy £1808.01. 05 pence
In all we think the church cost about £2,060.00.00

~15th May 1869

Saw Miss B - ugly old thing - dressed in the height of fashion, frilled blue petticoat, black satin pleat skirt, black bonnet with three different coloured roses and stuck up feathers like bottle brushes - such a guy! She offered to take us to the Horticultural but we would not go with her!

~Monday 15th 1870

We can think and talk only of Garibaldi and being wounded and a prisoner and in the hands of the Italian Government.

~April 5th Easter Sunday 1872

We have been working hard amongst the ruins of a Roman Villa - we have discovered on the Wadfield Farm - it appears to have been destroyed by fire owing to the quantities of wood ashes we found under the debris of walls. Nothing valuable has yet turned up, nothing but broken pottery, bricks, old nails, some old bolts and keys. The best thing we have found yet is part of a mosaic pavement which we have been trying for the last two days to remove by placing Plaster of Paris over it, a frame of wood round it, and then digging under it. I was very sorry for the men this afternoon when their longest piece gave way owing to them having hit something between the Plaster of Paris and the pavement, but the best parts are now removed and I have written to Minton's China works to ask if they can let me have pieces of red, white and yellow to restore it.

~26th December 1872
Red and scarlet cloaks are all the rage just now for ladies, I suppose because poor women will not wear them. Phillip was quite amused at my having had the courage to walk through the town in mine.

We are much interested also in reading Victor Hugo's "Les Miserables" a grand book full of photographic pictures of life - some call it an improper book - Heaven help them - they will read a horrid book called Barren Honor and see no harm in it!

~May 18th 1873
The family monument is now finished in Prestbury churchyard and it gives great satisfaction - it is by Mr. Phillip who did the marble work for us at Sudeley and the sculpture at the Albert Memorial.

~July 1873
When in London I saw Mr. William Morris the decorator and poet and asked his advice how to ornament a plain cottage ceiling - he advised it put in squares - a very old fashioned way revived he said - so the experiment is to be tried at Gretton in the new cottage.

~Oct 1873
To our regret and annoyance we find Mr. Jackson has appointed a ritualist to be curate - and to officiate of course in our little, but very Protestant churches of Sudeley and Gretton! We had such confidence in Mr. Jackson it seems too sad that it is now gone!

~November 5th 1873
Then to Silvy, the photographer, who paid me the greatest compliment by putting for a background a prison, a pocket handkerchief

in my hand and saying I looked exactly like Paul de la Roche's picture of Marie Antionette - one or two of the assistants came to look at me and as the resemblance has been frequently observed before, I suppose I may say my little vanity is greatly flattered.

~November -1873
Marianne, Miss Booth, Alfred, their groom and Catafago their courier have all started for the Nile!! Would that we were with them!

~November 1873
We have an artist from Worcester, a Mr. Rushton, taking our portraits, John with his hand on Juno's head, I feeding the beautiful white pigeons!

~November 1873
The Ashanti war has commenced the only one we know in it is young Alfred Charteris.

Alas! this week we have heard that poor young Alfred Charteris died in November of the cruel Gold Coast fever - he was buried at sea! but his father and mother had to learn this at Southampton whither they went to meet him!

~December 1873
We receive most delightful letters from Marianne - 150 miles below Cairo - they have fallen in with pleasant companions in Mr. McCullum, the Egyptian artist, and Miss Amelia Edwards the authoress and our acquaintance.

~May 1874
To Ems also in June and July with Peter - while there Marianne and Miss Booth came to us for a couple of days on their way home from the East! Their stories were most interesting and they looked as fresh and well as if they had just come from amongst the mountains! On their return to England they took their curiosities to the British Museum where they were all pronounced genuine! and they with glee went back to their Bagstones and haymaking and pigs and calves.

~July 1874

The children from the poor house are to attend our schools - those belonging to Winchcombe are to pay 3d, outsiders 6d per week - this is John's crotchet as he says the schools were not built for outsiders.

~Nov. 1874

Edith has been with me for several weeks - George Talbot of Guiting wants to marry her but he has so little, and William not inclined to do very much, I fear it will have to fall through! - but we must hope for the best.

There has been great talk about having Winchcombe supplied with water - and they want it from our St. Kenelm's Well. It would be a pity to disturb that - as there are so many other springs - they have had a meeting in Winchcombe about it - they all want water, but don't want to pay for it - Jackson the Parson and Plumbe the lawyer, announced a resolution in favour of a water supply. Smith Wood & Somebody altered it a little but which signified the same thing - the small rate payers then voted they didn't want it , and the meeting ended for the present in smoke!

~Nov 1874

William writes he is off to Guiting on his perilous journey! With power from Edith to decide as he thinks best! (clever little woman) He says if George Talbot is in earnest it will be a match.

~November 1874

Very sorry to leave Eastbourne - I go to the Midland to meet John who has come to take me home. William arrives at midnight - November 18th - direct from Temple Guiting where he met Miss Jane, George Talbot's father from Withington, & Mr. Hohler - they were all very much pleased with one another - and William has promised Edith a handsome allowance of £1,000 a year and the young people are to have an interview and talk over their own affairs and let him know if they think it will do!

~November 1874

Edith and George Talbot are engaged! May they ever be half as happy as they are now. Letters of congratulation are flowing in from all sides - Lord Shrewsbury writes "that if the young lady is half such a good fellow as her father, or Uncle Phillip she will do".

~November 1874
Tom is Mayor for Macclesfield and down third for Sheriff for Cheshire.

"A sense of duty pursues us ever; it is omnipresent like the Deity" Webster

~Sunday January 1875
I had 17 girls in my class at the Sunday School.

~February 1st 1875
A long time ago a beautiful ring was found near our Roman Villa remains. The British Museum and Castellani pronounced it a perfect specimen of an ancient Roman ring worn by some grandee of the period - a few days ago Mr. Plumbe our Winchcombe lawyer, was dining with his client Mr. Wilson at Bath, who was showing him some curious rings and remarked that he once lost a very nice old one in the neighbourhood of Winchcombe! Mr. Plumbe is inclined to think mine must be the missing one - it will be strange if it is - and still stranger if it is not.

~Thursday, August 10th 1876
William would not so much as go within the Tytherington gates - not even to see his little grandson when the Talbots went to stay there for the house warming.

"No", said William when we urged him to go in "No we have made one great mistake in building such a large house, do not let us make another by going into it"! - and so in time Mary, like a true heroine, packed up all again returned to Butley, closed Tytherington - and thus ended her dream - her great object of interest which has occupied so many years.

~February 1877
Johnny is at Hombury, recovering after his accident; Mr. Pearson heard it described at the club and that the gentleman who saw it in

the hunting field said he would have been killed but for the happy suggestion of a young farmer who said get a saddle off one of the horses and stick it on the gentleman's head. This was done and the horse removed from over him, where they lay in the ditch together. The horse naturally struggled violently, and the saddle was cut to pieces!

~February 1877
Colonel Gordon is at Cairo - he is made Governor of the Sudan - absolute and uncontrolled - the Sudan is supposed to mean from the second cataract as far away as anyone can go South and West, a country larger than England and crossed in every direction by slave dealers, whose destruction is his great object in life - an appointment perilous though glorious. Colonel Gordon has taken an immense fancy to Johnny and wishes to get leave of absence for him - for twelve months from Duke of Cambridge to whom he has telegraphed for the same - he seems also to have taken a great liking to Marianne and Miss Booth. Marianne describes him as a very gentle, quiet, dreamy little man.

~1877-8
As I went to the morning Sunday School the Castle field looked powdered with gold - the buttercups had opened all their leaves before the first really Summer's sun. I gave my girls a lesson on law, duty - work - industry and talent. Life of George Stevenson - I gave them each a scrap book with pictures in and to encourage them to be tidy and take care of their cards.

~1877
A dreary sermon from the vicar on the rich man and Lazarus. "Not much hope for the rich - not much for the poor".

~1877
For the first time I have discovered our Sudeley boys are trying to make arrow heads. Hitherto the collection of flints has gone on well and innocent of forgery. This evening two - were brought evidently chipped in the inner part to make them look more like arrowheads. These are the first it is curious how soon the slightest chipping is perceptible on the flints.

Line upon Line Gibraltar

~Thursday 21st March 1877

John writes from Ems that Wm. Spencer Walpole and Lady Simon are both there which makes it pleasant for him - he is taking the cure in earnest - no Russians there this year - the German perception is that the Russians will take as much of Asia as they want then make peace. Wagner is also there - a queer looking fellow and being a musician cannot stand the Band!

~Monday 25th March 1877

On the new mare to take a copy of my Annals to John and William Staite whose family for 7 years lived on the Lodge Farm. I have received many nice and complimentary letters on the subject of the Annals from Lord Beauchamp and Hertford, the Bishop, Mr. Borlase, and Dr. Bully.

~Wednesday 5th July 1877

I went to meet two workman to discuss what could be done with the Elizabethan House, opposite the church - now our property - my idea is to improve it and make it interesting both within and without - to restore the old mantlepiece of stone - the windows etc - and have a museum in the lower rooms - Pearson the carpenter said he remembered when it was used as Alms houses!

~1877

In the Chandos Room I have arranged in a case some old head-dresses, my own wedding wreath of orange blossom, a large cushion shaped cap covered with little gold plates - which must have looked like a shower of gold when new, perhaps 200 years ago. Near it I have placed an exquisitely embroidered baby's cap - embroidered for me when it was rumoured, but alas without foundation, that I was going to have a child - there is something very touching about that little cap which brings tears into my eyes - as I remember a few years ago being affected in seeing in a collection of needlework at the South Kensington some baby garments made by the Princess Elizabeth for the expected infant of her sister Queen Mary!

~August 1877

Lady Elcho one day sent over all their servants - indoors and outdoors - they had their picnic and were then taken over the Castle.

~August 1877

Mr. Wyatt, the architect, has been with us planning and scheming what is to be done with the old house opposite the church, so as to add out-buildings without destroying the character of the old house.

~Sunday 16th September 1877

30 years today have we been wed! What a lifetime to look forward to what a speck to look back upon. It seems "but the other day" our Wedding day and all the guests assembled - and the thousands of kind faces that smiled on us as we went to the parish church at Prestbury - and my dear mother - and how I never saw her again after that day. We parted at the door on the stairs in the front hall at Hurdsfield. She could not bear to come to the church.

The old mother church at Prestbury is to be restored under Sir Gilbert Scott where we have all been married, and many buried, so I have volunteered £100 which gives great satisfaction.

~October 1877

I am much interest in " The Paddington and Parisian Laundry" lately remodelled by our friend Miss Amelia B. Edwards and others - it is at the old manor house, Paddington - 70 French & English laundry maids kept all clean & happy. Marianne and I have taken shares in it, she to the extent of £50 I only for £20!

~October 1877

Johnny has been spending a few days with us on his way to the Duke of Beauforts - a curious and somewhat interesting specimen of the tribe of "The Royal Horse Guards"! Clothes superlative, boots - oh ye gods what fits! what expanse of shirt front when dressed for dinner - how careful at dinner not to partake of fattening food! I was afraid he was not well, his Uncle Dent said "it was only damned affectation!"

The Ramble Barcelona

Valencia. The Alameda

Mr. Newman sends me word from Constantinople that my dona-tion of £100 to the Turkish fund is to go in tobacco. Half to be sent to the front, half to be reserved for the sufferers in hospital where it will be of the greatest comfort, when limbs are amputated or balls extracted - she was conversing with Dr. Milligen (Byron's physician in Greece!) - he said also that Tobacco was the greatest boon that could be bestowed upon them!

~May 2nd 1878

In Alms Houses I saw five of the inmates who all thanked me for having the bells put up in their bedrooms.

~1879

On the 16th Mr. & Mrs. Wedgewood left us after having been our guests for ten days - during that time we went to the Aquarium and, were charmed and surprised with the intelligence of the sea lions - heard a lecture on electric light by Professor Pepper - saw him burn a diamond! We lunched with the Stevensons.

~1879

MAY DAY - a snowstorm in the morning and in the afternoon.

~May 3rd 1879

Long conversation with housekeeper Bayliss who told me many discouraging things of the ingratitude of Winchcombe people - I said how I had loved, prayed for, worked for, and devoted myself to Winchcombe and I did not think there was any love in return.
She said when Prince Albert was alive no one thought anything of him - now he was dead, enough could not be said in his praise! I thought it a very pretty way for a servant to put it.

~July 26th 1878

A dreadful storm came on at 4 o'clock just as we were going into the long room - one flash was terrific - at 10 minutes past 4 it killed a cow in the Boilingwell Orchard and our poor Tom Shotten - jack of all trades who was carrying the milk from the farm for our guests was struck down into the hedge and narrowly escaped with his life. I do not remember so bad a storm since about 1850 when we were visiting the Uncles Dent in August. After long dry weather the rain flowed in thro' doors and windows. When it was over, as we thought, I opened the billiard room window and looked out - a flash came from over Postlip which seemed to be coming direct upon me - when it suddenly turned attracted by the lightning conductor. With it came the thunder sounding like a hundred canon balls! The lightning struck the tower loosening several large stones of the dungeon!

~1878
Mr. George Barnard, of the Bank of England has sent me a piece of lace which his wife inherited from her family of Lawsons, descended from Queen Katherine Parr - the tradition with it was that it had belonged to Anne Boleyn and had been the lace canopy carried over Princess Elizabeth at her christening - so I have purchased it for £25 - on further examining it we discovered that Anne Boleyn's crest and monogram are worked in the lace - and repeated again and again. The falcon on a golden perch with roses, Tudor and Lancaster and York - a very interesting addition to our historic relics.

In London I took it to the South Kensington where Mr. George Hallis was much interested in it - the emblem he said was perfectly correct. 40 years ago he had taken the trouble to make drawings in the British Museum of the emblems of all the different Queens, promising some day to send me a copy of the falcon peculiar to Anne Boleyn.

Johnny and his wife staying at the Duke of Beauforts to offer themselves for a week's hunting at Sudeley - to bring six horses - which would involve we suppose three or four grooms besides his valet and her maid - John not well enough to be at home - this proposition gave him something of an alarm - and we were obliged to decline them. We think also their servants coming from such an establishment as the Duke's would have been very discontented with the simple arrangements and frugal fare of our little menage!

~1878

My photograph taken by Silvy in 1866 - thought to be very like me - at the same time he took one standing with pocket handkerchief in hand, which he thought resembled that of Marie Antionette by De la Roche. I believe Silvy was killed in the Franco German war.

~1878

This represents my dear little grey ponies and carriage which I bought from Dr. & Mrs. Bully (of Cheltenham College).

~Summer, 1878

In the evening we drove out 2 miles to see the 48 Druid stones. everything was bathed in beauty.

~November 1879

When I was found lamenting over poor Juno's sufferings, many expressed surprise that I should be so much concerned as they said, for, "only a dog"! She lies buried under the Mulberrry tree my sister and I planted by the Dungeon Tower nearly twenty years ago.

"Only a dog"! but my tears fall fast
When I think you'll soon lie in your grave
My tears fall fast, when I think of the past
Poor Juno! so noble and brave

"Only a dog" - but my heart nigh breaks
At your patient endurance of pain -
Gentle and quiet as if for our sakes
You could suffer as much again

"Only a dog" with that loving eye
Beaming upon me with faith and trust
(Humbly expressed in that muffled cry)
That assuage her great pain I must!

PEDOMETER TELLS FOR 1879 THAT I HAVE WALKED
1,140 MILES.

Miss Maggs has presented to "The Castle" an exquisite little brooch containing some of Queen Katherine Parr's hair - Q.K.P's gold monogram, surrounded with the smallest pearls. The golden colour hair is terminated with the finest gold fringe.

It was bequeathed to Miss Maggs by Miss Durham of Postlip - her brother was one of the band who so roughly treated the Queen's coffin - the hair in the brooch having been taken from the Royal remains at that time.

It is a very valuable addition to the treasures in the Queen's Room. It is said in Winchcombe by those who remember the stories of the last generations that all who shared in the abominable transactions, met with sudden and untimely deaths. This Mr. Durham poisened himself!

~July 26th 1880

It was very disappointing to find William was after all unseated for Macclesfield - after 49 years electioneering. I suppose the bribery was too transparent and the committee only too careless.

~August 4th 1880

My maid Elizabeth heard the "death watch" for the first time and that night Edwin Pardington died at the Boilingwell. The next night John heard it in his little sitting room for the first time in his life - called me in to hear it - the next morning we heard of the sudden death of Mr. Jones's brother-in-law, at the Almsbury Farm. Mr. Jones, Mayor of Worcester, - and this morning General Hinde writes to tell us his second boy Charlie is among the "missing" after the last disastrous affair in India.

~1880

French Dressing Room - put up little white bed - I gave Edith a long time ago - faded pieces of old silk we brought from Florence, lilac blue chintz - white and gold brackets - shelves, washstand, bidet, give it quite a comfortable and dainty look - crimson curtains also not before they were wanted.

French Bedroom - a new dark carpet replaces a handsome old Aubusson which has been killing the tapestry ever since the old Uncles put it there.

In Chinese Room - I have put little black chest of drawers - easy black and blue chair - bonnet box - ottoman - little black table - lowered one of the Chinese solid chairs.

Cumnor Dressing Room - New Turkey carpet - bed - hung up a few pictures - washstand we brought from Antwerp. Wardrobe I bought from Askews in Brighton - Cumnor Room new carpet in place of heavy rugs.

The French Room - re-arranged furniture and brought all a little more into harmony - towel rails in all the rooms made after my own design - we consider a success.

North Room Re-arranged with a view to economy of space - blue china and black brackets put up - matting on washstands put on for effect - wardrobe in dressing room I bought from Mr. Askew in Brighton - wonderful fit - also little Dutch shelf from Ghent for china & hanging a great success.

PEDOMETER TELLS ME I HAVE WALKED
920 MILES THIS YEAR 1880
- 180 LESS THAN LAST YEAR.

~30th January 1881
Accomplished a good days work in changing the rooms for paying the road men from the Public House to the Coffee Tavern.
There were unusually large numbers to receive their money - and many had hot cocoa and bread and butter instead of beer.

~January 1881
One of our cottagers was killed at Gretton, jumping off the wagon his smock must have caught - he fell on his head, cutting it against a sharp piece of blue stone - he was dead in a few minutes - a very nice boy of 14 Mr. Fred Lanchborough of the Parkes Cottages - has

many times brought me flints he has found up on the hill - he looks quite beautiful taking his rest, so lifelike still.

~March 3rd 1881
Cousin Tom being in America - he kindly sends me stamps for my collection - some obtained from General Hazen - the head of the Post Office department to whom he had a letter of introduction from Sir Edward Thornton - some are "specimen stamps" and therefore unique - he says there is nothing worth buying in America which is a comfort except some Indian scalps lately taken from the heads of Sitting Bull's tribe by the Sioux.

~May Day - 1881
No snow for a wonder - First blue curtain finished of old work transferred - curtains from Harvey - the retired butcher's sister - she inherited them from her grand or great grandmother.

~7th May 1881
We buried our housekeeper Bayliss in Winchcombe churchyard. Our servants attending - I stood in the church porch with Mr. Jackson and placed on the coffin, when it was removed from the hearse, a lovely cross & wreath of flowers - she came as my maid nearly 30 years ago.

~May 10th 1881
John writes from London that Gladstone is threatened with paralysis - is very irritable - does not know what to be at - specially in the Bradlaugh difficulty.

~May 24th 1881
The country just now is so lovely I cannot make up my mind to go to London - the wallflowers are out now, the hawthorn and laburnums.

~25th May 1881
Finished arranging my arrowheads last week - coins and tokens finished today - the cases are a great success.

Valencia

First Experience in a Tartana. (which is without springs)

Bailen

~June 18th 1881

A small "grinding mill" arrived from Jerusalem for the museum, besides many other interesting objects for the Biblical illustrations.

~19th June 1881

Arranging design for the Vane on Chapel tower. Mr. Wyatt says my idea is unique and original and is much pleased with it.

~December 1881

William is working very hard to get the severe punishment pronounced on "Mair & May" mitigated - 9 months imprisonment - not first class!

~20th December 1881

John's birthday 63. May he have many returns of the day!

~24th December 1881

From Constantinople the news that the Jewish missionary, Mr. Newman is dead. After a few days illness at Haskioi. His last words were "Jesus" and "Jerusalem". I am so glad I knew him and seen his schools.

~1881

CHRISTMAS at Malvern - John and I. A sad letter from William who is very down about the Macclesfield lawyers being in prison - he feels isolated compared to what it was 30 or 40 years ago when we were a large and united family - and our elders still in the front! The ties seem to be loosening, every year more and more as Xmas comes round. The ground loosening under our feet as if preparing to receive us!

~December 1881

We have had all our cottagers to tea and given them their petticoats and presents - with others, including cottagers, making up 100 presents has made me very busy.

I find I have walked during the year about 700 miles!
We have "entertained" since March as follows

At Breakfast 175 times
At Luncheon 386
At Dinner 252
At Tea 1058 times.

~March 1883

I am presenting a statue of Queen Victoria in stone, by Mr. Boulton of Cheltenham to Macclesfield.

~March 4th 1883

News came of the Queen's escape from death by the hands of the assassin. John went down to Winchcombe and ordered the bells to be rung - shame to our rector and his curate - they took no notice of this on Sunday 5th and returned no thanksgiving.

~Saturday 11th March 1883

Roman remains - a pavement, walls, etc., found in Spoonley Coppice.

~Sat. 11th March 1883

I have just purchased The Gate public house for £700 which is to be closed and we shall try and convert it into a temperance Inn.

~April 9th 1883

Decided upon an American typewriter £21.

~April 9th 1883

Saw Sarah Bernhardt at the theatre and was much disappointed in her - the piece very poor in plot.

~April 16th 1883

Took MB to see Irving and Ellen Terry in Romeo & Juliet - most beautifully put upon the stage.

~13th March 1884

To an interesting meeting at 104 Jermyn St. For the Prevention of Cruelty to Animals - Baroness B. Coutts should have been in the chair.

Professor Koch has great credit for having discovered the Cholera microbe - he calls himself "an observer not a healer" and the man who discovers how to destroy the microbe will be the greatest benefactor.

This was the last Christmas "we" spent together at Hurdsfield!! I shall never go there again - my brother (unworthy of the name brother) has never since invited me - banished from my own dear old home - and the family, brothers, sister & nephews - yes nephews! who have never moved a straw to make an opening for me.

A cold North East wind - bright morning. I joined him in his little study with Mr. Cox - I sat with them for some time - Mr. C. advised his going out in the sheltered quadrangle - he was at his work and interviewing people till late in the afternoon - then he walked as far as Pardingtons with Duke and Busy - everybody who met him said how ill he looked and that he could not be long for this world - he seemed better at dinner and we had a long talk, curiously about his will, heirs, property, nephews, Hindes, his uncles, Johnny, also at luncheon we had a long talk on much similar subjects - I told him my scheme for the £10 deposit fund, he said it was surrounded with difficulties but that he has left a legacy of £5 to each inmate of the Alms houses for 3 years - at 8.30 he went to the study - about 8.50 I took Busy to him - he was singing to himself - it sounded cheerful but I have wondered since if it meant pain - at 9.30 he came into the little library saying he was going to bed and sat down for a last chat as he often did - quite cheerful - then he took up his bed candle - saying he supposed I should not follow for 2 or 3 hours - a few minutes after he knocked for me from his room above - I thought the knocking somehow different from usual and I rushed upstairs - he was rubbing favourite oils on his chest, and complaining of a return of the pain which seized him the previous week - after the oils he asked me to keep quite quiet. He said he was foolish to have gone out in the cold wind - I was very anxious to ring and tell someone to fetch the doctor but was afraid to fidget him - he drew the bedclothes well over his shoulders, said he should soon be better when he was warmer - did not seem in acute pain (at least I hope not) I remained quiet at the dressing table - he said "Oh Nem this pain"! he turned round as if to compose himself for sleep - gave one loud breath which made me think he had fallen asleep, the second alarmed me, the third I looked at him when alas, alas, alas, he was gone!

~1885
From March 25th to October 25th seven long sad months of utter loneliness - darkness - misery - sorrow - so suddenly to lose my dear husband - the constant companion of 38 years - the one to whom I looked up to for everything - the one whose will was my will - whose pleasure was my pleasure - now I have no one to live for - to consult - to take interest in - to please - no one to live for me or take a real interest in anything that concerns my health or happiness - no one to talk things over with! Oh it is all a darkness that may be felt - the Past is like a happy dream - the Present, work and toil without object or interest - the Future, a lonely, lonely journey - and when all is over the Hope, the blessed Hope, of a joyful eternity!

~Aug. 9th 1886
Workmen are pegging out and preparing for the new West buildings - a great undertaking for me all alone - but with Mr. Wyatt to the front and the shadow of Sir Gilbert Scott in the background I feel that every stone will be in accordance with what my dear husband would approve.

~Jan. 16th 1887

I find last year I stepped 1,075 miles	
my guests were at breakfast	284
at luncheon	468
at dinner	380
at tea	645

~March 5th 1887

My Birthday - once more without my husband!! how lonely - without a single remembrance from brother, sister or nephew! Pretty verses written by a homely friend in Winchcombe, and baskets of wild flowers from the School children - but what are they to the loving words of former years!

~March 1887

William & Fitz have been opening a democratic club in Macclesfield of which the 1st rule is to work for the abolition of the House of Lords in England and establishment of Parliament in Dublin! William writes to me: "I don't see why you should aim to do just what the old Dents and John would be supposed to wish" - he goes on to explain the changes that have been made during the last few years. How such sentiments would have grieved them all but in William, & Peter who not only thought it but acted it! I am glad the name of Brocklehurst is not to be held here!

~March 1887

Mr. Cattermole's picture and sketch have arrived - the picture is hung in the Hall. It represents William Dent starting as High Sheriff in 1851 to meet the judges at Overbridge - accompanied by 300 friends, neighbours and tenants - (the portraits have to be finished as I want the 3 uncles represented and my husband.) They all stand at the door - I feel a pleasure in thinking how gratified the kind old man would have felt in knowing that wonderful day was immortalised in one of Mr. Cattermole's pictures! and here comes in the void not having one left to whom I may tell the pleasure!

~June 18th 1888

I return home after a month at Ilfracombe with Miss Crane and the Stantons - hot water laid on in all the downstairs rooms - wonderful improvement.

~August 22nd 1888

Flower Show - more than 2,000 people here - a lovely day - and the improvements all looked their best.

The Malaguena
Baile del Paes Savilla

~September 23rd 1888
Garden opened - 200 came - next Sunday dull day - not so many.

~October 1st 1888
Covered walk nearly finished - windows in Lodge gate made with larger frames - the workmen have been so obstinate in not letting me have my way about them!

~October 3rd 1888
Smallpox in Winchcombe - 10 cases in all brought of course from the Paper Mills.

~October 4th 1888
Arranging for the stream - covered way - trees and hedges to be cut down - & open views - Indoors arranged cases of "family shoes" & foreign ones collected abroad.

~24th November 1888
I have purchased cottages from Stephens the Clerk, at the bottom of Duck Street on the right hand side - may be useful some day if a new drive is made to Sudeley.

~December 1888
Mr. Jackson begs I will build him a Rectory for Sudeley - not very likely after all his cruel and ungrateful conduct to my husband, his best friend!

1888 I have walked 1,160 miles
my guests were at breakfast   522
at luncheon   630
at dinner   595
at tea   933

~1889
These beautiful lines come from one who had known me long, and now urged me to be his wife - for a few hours I hesitated - it was a temptation to go out of my utter loneliness into sunshine, to

be surrounded by love & sympathy - but 2 years my junior & his wealth and position seemed likely to bring upon me more responsibilities - and of these I already have too many - forsaken by those I would have most leaned upon William and Mary, the Talbots - and shut out from my own dear home thro' the caprice of a cruel, selfish, brother - it does not bear thinking about.

~4th March 1889
Busy planting the Sentinel trees by the moat and Lodge in place of the cedars which died owing to their being too large for removal.

~5th March 1889
I am 66 today! God forgive me if I somewhat repine at my utter loneliness - for not a little word of remembrance or love have I from brother, or sister, nephew or niece! The grave has robbed me of all my love.

~April 1st 1889
I am venturing to decorate a little the iron work over the covered way putting bosses and spears of a lighter shade to the ground, blacking nails of the girders etc. - very difficult to decorate.

~September 18th 1889
My poor dear faithful Duke went to the happy hunting ground - a good age for a Mastiff - who can say how I shall miss him and his loving welcome - when there was no one else he was too big for the parlour so never admitted in former times. They buried him under the Mulberry tree.

~September 29th 1889
A good day's work planted an avenue of Cedars by the moat and Lime trees by the drive.

~December 24th 1889
Poor little Busy was so ill - I had her put out of her misery - she had some internal complaint and was incurable - 14 years. The little faithful creature was seldom out of my sight - now both my best friends are gone! They really were my best friends.

~January 17th 1890

Very much interested with my plan for alterations in stable yard for putting coal and coke underground.

~July 10th 1890

The exterior of the North tower completed - looks very new now - quite an eyesore - but in a few years it will be toned down and will be a great improvement to the Castle.

Letter from Drayton Wyatt - the Architect I also returned Mr. Oakey's "nice note". His work at Sudeley has throughout been done, I believe, carefully, and well, and substantially; thanks, in a great measure, no doubt, to the "Factotum";- not forgetting, however, that I always made a point that everything should be clearly understood beforehand, either by drawing, instructions, or both. Hence, happily, all has been carried on without any hitch; and if all the parties who have been concerned in the same are now satisfied, what more can be wished!

~November 3rd 1890

I had a large mass of Portugal laurels cut down which had outgrown their place - the view from study window much lightened in consequence - a door now shows in the wall which was blocked up some years ago - and through which George III passed several times - an apricot tree was planted there to commemorate his coming - it is now to be renewed.

~November 4th 1890

I began to collect superstitions of this district for the Winchcombe leaflet.

~November 8th 1890

I had the proposed new bridge put up in wood to see the effect.

~November 18th 1891

Avenue of Beeches planted! They will grow up and cast their pretty shadows and spread out their arms to catch the rays of sun - and men and women will walk by them, children will play under them, but there will be no one to remember the old lady who lovingly planted them, always in memory of those who are gone.

```
1891 I have walked 1,134 miles
my guests were at breakfast  500
at luncheon                  604
at dinner                    596
at tea                     1,491
```

I arranged for American Flag to be up to commemorate the discovery of America!

```
1893 I have walked 1,146 miles
my guests were at breakfast  658
at luncheon                1,164
at dinner                    795
at tea                     1,385
```

~April 1894
Got up the courage to go to London - the first time since I have been left alone - to a Ladies' Club - curious place at 22 Gratton Road. During my four days stay I visited my dentist - Mr. Coffin - four times - two visits to the oculist - Mr. Nettleship - who said my cataract was ready to be removed - (he's lately been very successful in removing one from Mr. Gladstone's eye). To Dr. Charles Phillips for my leg - that was sprained at Weymouth and a second damage following in consequence of the abominable cement pavement put down in Winchcombe, contrary to all propriety and taste.

~May 15th 1894
About 40 members of the British Medical Society lunched - went over the Castle - some walked in the Roman Villa - some talked - one old fellow said speaking of hereditary, "that sometimes it went so far that wooden legs even ran in families" - I replied I had often heard of wooden heads running in families but never wooden legs.

~April 22nd 1894
Our Flower Show and Easter Exhibition - old barn roofed in cost me nearly £100.

~May 1st 1895
Went to London - at 30 Cambridge Terrace - where Agnes Jones met me - and was my bodyguard during the time I was in Mr. Nettleship's hands - he removed cataract from right eye on the 6th, a beautiful and painless operation - I watched every movement and was delighted to see a blue speck of light as soon as it was cleared - I was allowed to come home in a fortnight on the 22nd - they rang the Church bells for my happy return and success of operation.

1895 I have walked 1,200 miles	
my guests were at breakfast	416
at luncheon	482
at dinner	615
at tea	2,109